Fantastic Frogs

Penelope Arlon

MCL FOR
NEPTUNE CITY
PUBLIC LIBRARY

SCHOLASTIC INC.

New York   Toronto   London   Auckland
Sydney   Mexico City   New Delhi   Hong Kong

Read more! Do more!

After you read this book, download your free all-new digital activities.

You can show what a great reader you are!

For Mac and PC

Take quizzes about the fun facts in this book!

Play frog games and activities with videos and sounds!

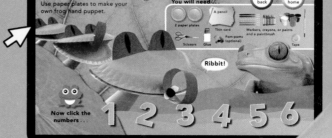

Log on to

www.scholastic.com/discovermore/readers

Enter this special code: **L2CWNR6XCCK2**

Contents

EDUCATIONAL BOARD:
Monique Datta, EdD, Asst. Professor, Rossier School of Education, USC;
Karyn Saxon, PhD, Elementary Curriculum Coordinator, Wayland, MA;
Francie Alexander, Chief Academic Officer, Scholastic Inc.

Copyright © 2013 by Scholastic Inc.

All rights reserved. Published by Scholastic Inc., *Publishers since 1920.*
SCHOLASTIC, SCHOLASTIC DISCOVER MORE™, and associated logos are trademarks
and/or registered trademarks of Scholastic Inc.

No part of this publication may be reproduced, stored in a retrieval system,
or transmitted in any form or by any means, electronic, mechanical, photocopying,
recording, or otherwise, without written permission of the publisher.
For information regarding permission, write to Scholastic Inc.,
Attention: Permissions Department, 557 Broadway, New York, NY 10012.

ISBN (Trade) 978-0-545-57271-2
ISBN (Clubs) 978-0-545-66125-6

12 11 10 9 8 7 6 5 4 3 2 1   13 14 15 16 17 18/0

Printed in the U.S.A.   40
This edition first printing, December 2013

Scholastic is constantly working to lessen the environmental
impact of our manufacturing processes. To view our
industry-leading paper procurement policy,
visit www.scholastic.com/paperpolicy.

All about frogs

Listen! Was that a croak? Look! Was that a wave in the water? Can you spot a frog? All around you, frogs are hanging out in damp places.

Green tree frog

Edible frog

African clawed frog

Tree frog

Ornate horned frog

It's a fact!

In 2012, a new kind of frog wa

Frogs are amphibians.
They live two lives.
Frogs live in water
and they live on land.

Red-eyed tree frog

Poison dart frog

Glass frog

Marsh frog

Imbabura tree frog

Bullfrog

Malayan horned frog

...ound in New York. It's called a tree leopard frog.

5

Amazing bodies

Adult frogs use lungs to breathe, like you do. Frogs also breathe through their skin! Their skin must stay damp for them to breathe. That's why they look for wet places.

Toads and frogs are both amphibians.

A toad's skin has bumps. It is drier than a frog's skin.

Frogs make sticky slime
to help keep their skin damp.
Frogs can pull off old skin to show
new skin. Then they eat the old skin!

Frogs are small animals. Danger hides in the water and on land. Frogs use their senses to spot danger. Their bodies help them hop away or hide from hungry predators.

Strong legs are ready to leap. In a second, a frog can jump away from danger.

It's a fact!

Some frogs scare predators with their smelly

The frog can spot trouble with its big eyes. It has three eyelids on each eye!

NEW WORD

predator
PRED-uh-tur
A **predator** hunts down and eats another animal.

SAY IT OUT LOUD

Behind the eye, the ear listens for sounds.

Sticky toe pads help the frog hang on to leaves.

:kin. Spadefoot toads smell like peanut butter!

9

Quick! A frog needs to get away!
It jumps on its strong back legs. It
can leap more than 20 times its
own length. When it
reaches water,
it dives in.

Other animals
have webbed
feet, too.

Duck

Otter

The frog swims fast. It uses its webbed feet to push itself through the water.

Webbed toes push away more water than toes alone do.

Poison dart frogs

If a frog can't get away, it may have other ways to stay safe. Poison dart frogs are brightly colored. This warns enemies that they are poisonous.

Tomato frog

A tomato frog can puff up its body to look larger than it really is.

It's a fact!

A drop of poison from the golden

A gray tree frog can change color to match bark.

Many frogs use camouflage. They blend in with their backgrounds. Where are the frogs hiding? Can you find them?

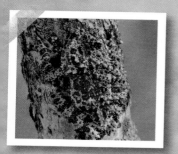

poison frog can kill ten people.

Eat up!

Frogs eat other animals, like bugs and worms. With big eyes, this frog watches for prey. Here's a cricket! The frog's long, sticky tongue flicks out. The cricket is stuck. It is swallowed whole. The frog blinks. Its eyeballs help push the food down its throat.

A bullfrog will eat anything it can swallow.

A green tree frog snacks on a worm.

An African bullfrog swallows a rat. Its eyeballs move back to help it swallow.

Yummy fly!

Tadpole to frog

Most frogs hatch from eggs in water. A frog lives the first part of its life as a tadpole. It then goes through a change, called metamorphosis.

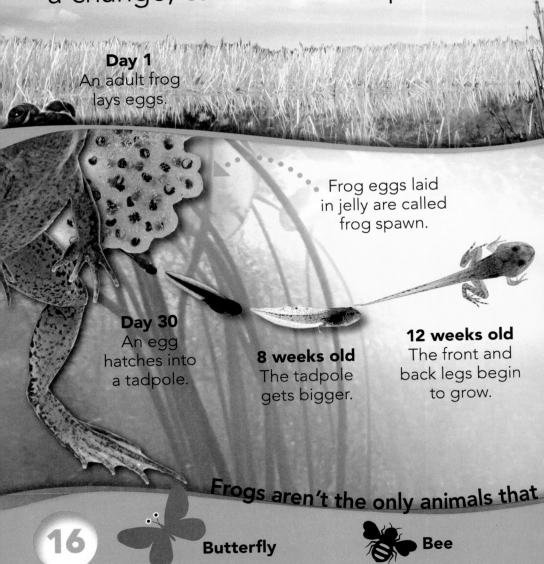

Day 1
An adult frog lays eggs.

Frog eggs laid in jelly are called frog spawn.

Day 30
An egg hatches into a tadpole.

8 weeks old
The tadpole gets bigger.

12 weeks old
The front and back legs begin to grow.

Frogs aren't the only animals that

Butterfly

Bee

It turns into an adult frog. An adult frog spends the rest of its life on land and in water.

14 weeks old
The long tail starts to get smaller.

16 weeks old
The froglet climbs out of the water.

Adult
The fully grown frog can now live on land.

NEW WORD

metamorphosis
met-uh-MOR-fuh-sis
After **metamorphosis**, a frog looks very different!

SAY IT OUT LOUD

go through metamorphosis!

 Ladybug

Crab

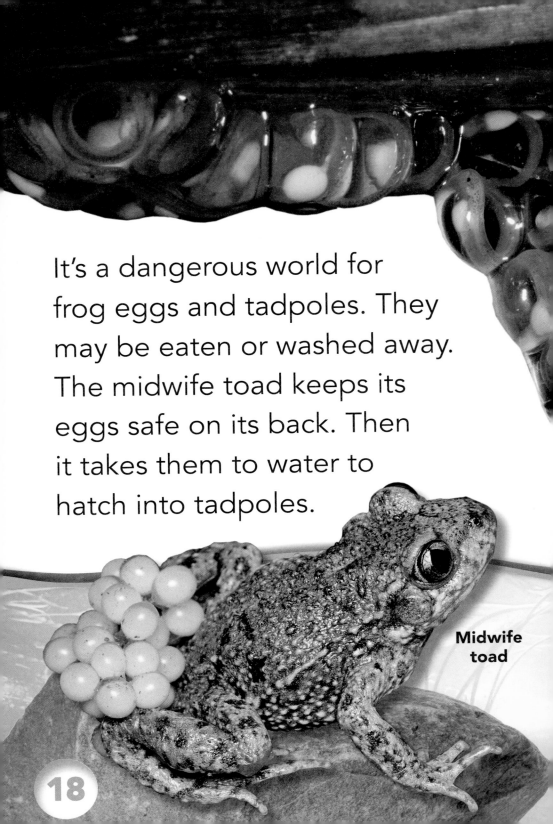

It's a dangerous world for frog eggs and tadpoles. They may be eaten or washed away. The midwife toad keeps its eggs safe on its back. Then it takes them to water to hatch into tadpoles.

Midwife toad

Glass frog

The glass frog lays its eggs under a branch hanging over a river. The male guards the eggs. When they hatch, the tadpoles drop into the water!

Tadpoles are kept here.

Darwin's frogs keep tadpoles safe in their throats!

Sky-blue poison frogs carry their tadpoles on their backs.

Look out for frogs

Frogs live almost all over the world. They do not live in Antarctica. Frogs have ways of living in tough places. In the desert,

The wood frog lives in the cold Arctic.

NORTH AMERICA

EUROPE

AFRICA

SOUTH AMERICA

The poison dart frog lives in the rainforest.

The bullfrog lives in swamps and ponds.

The desert rain frog lives by the sea. It stays wet from sea fog.

frogs rest in the ground for months. They wake up when the rains come. In the Arctic winter, the wood frog freezes like a piece of ice. It warms up again in the spring!

The agile frog is a great color for hiding in forests.

ASIA

AUSTRALASIA

The corroboree frog lives in the mountains.

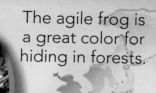

The Wallace's flying frog lives in the rainforest. It glides from tree to tree.

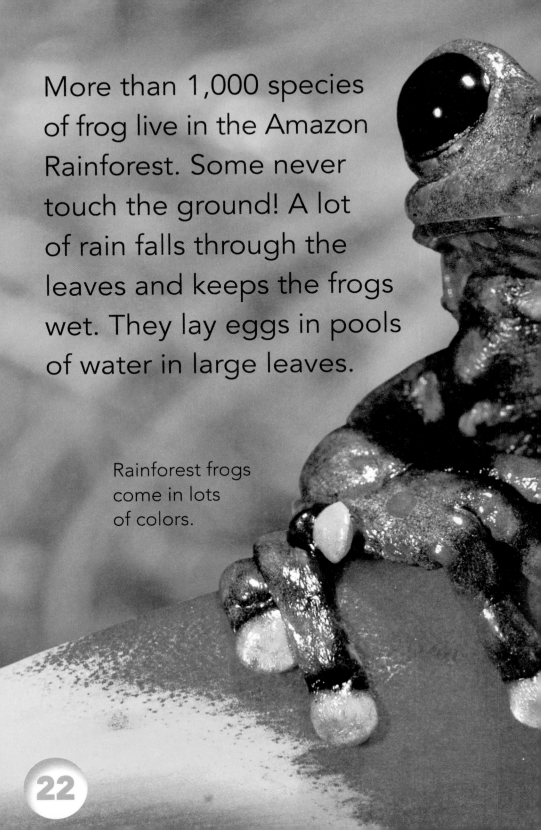

More than 1,000 species of frog live in the Amazon Rainforest. Some never touch the ground! A lot of rain falls through the leaves and keeps the frogs wet. They lay eggs in pools of water in large leaves.

Rainforest frogs come in lots of colors.

NEW WORD
species
SPEE-sheez
Animals that have babies together are usually from the same **species**.
SAY IT OUT LOUD

Rio Chingual Valley tree frog

23

Frogs in trouble

There are millions of frogs in the wild. About 1,900 species are in danger of becoming extinct, or dying out. There are three main

Fewer trees
The peat swamp frog is losing its home. Many trees have been cut down in the rainforest where it lives.

Poisoned rivers
The Limosa harlequin frog is being poisoned. Humans have harmed its river home with waste.

reasons: Rainforests are being cut down. Humans have poisoned rivers with waste. And many frogs are dying from a disease.

Sick frogs
There are no more gastric brooding frogs. They all died from a disease.

NEW WORD
extinct
ik-STINGKT
A kind of animal is **extinct** if no more animals of that type are still living.
SAY IT OUT LOUD

25

Many people are working to save frogs. One team in Sri Lanka builds paths for frogs! People make ponds in different parts of the rainforest. Then they make paths between the ponds. The frogs use the paths to move to new, safer areas.

These frogs are all Sri Lankan shrub frogs.

Charith Senanayake works to help frogs in the rainforest of Sri Lanka. "Frogs can tell us about the health of all the rainforest plants and animals. Frogs don't often like to live in polluted areas. So lots of healthy frogs equals a healthy forest!"

Sri Lanka

Record-breaking frogs

There are almost 6,000 species of frog. Check out 10 of the coolest!

1 Deadliest frog
Some people use the poison from poison dart frogs for hunting.

3 Biggest frog
The goliath frog can grow to more than 1 foot long!

4 Smallest frog
A 0.2-inch-long frog has been found. That's really tiny!

2 Weirdest frog
The Surinam toad has a very flat body.

5 Best at disappearing
Glass frogs have see-through skin.

6 Bumpiest skin
The Vietnamese mossy frog is covered in lumps and bumps. It looks just like a handful of moss.

9 Rainiest frogs
In 2005, some frogs got sucked into the air during a storm. Then they rained back down!

7 Noisiest tadpoles
The tadpoles of the ornate horned frog are the only tadpoles that we know of that make sounds.

Eek!

8 Best jumper
The red-eyed tree frog can jump 150 times its body length.

10 Loudest frog
The male coqui has a noisy squeak that is as loud as a chain saw!

Glossary

amphibian
An animal that lives in water when it is young, and both in water and on land when it is an adult.

blink
To close and open the eyes very quickly.

camouflage
Natural coloring that helps animals blend in with what is around them.

croak
The sound that a frog makes.

damp
Slightly wet.

disease
A sickness.

extinct
No longer found alive.

flick
To move quickly and sharply.

glide
To move through air or water smoothly and easily.

hatch
To be born by breaking out of an egg.

lung
An organ inside a human or animal that fills with air when it breathes.

metamorphosis
A change that some animals go through as they become adults.

poison
A substance that can kill or hurt a person, plant, or animal.

polluted
Made dirty.

predator
An animal that hunts other animals for food.

prey
An animal that is hunted by another animal for food.

rainforest
A wet, tropical forest.

species
A group into which animals of the same type are sorted.

swallow
To make food or drink move from the mouth to the stomach.

swamp
An area of wet land.

tadpole
A young frog that lives in water and has a tail. When it is very young, it has no legs.

waste
Trash.

webbed
Having toes that are connected by folds of skin.

Here are the hidden frogs from page 13:

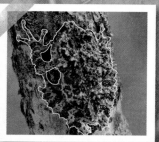

Index

Image credits
Photography and artwork
1 (main image): Minden Pictures/SuperStock; 1 (background): Wtolenaars/Dreamstime; 2 (computer monitor): skodonnell/iStockphoto; 2 (frogs around computer): kerkla/iStockphoto, GlobalP/iStockphoto, Antagain/iStockphoto; 2 (arrows): pagadesign/iStockphoto; 2 (standing frog cl): Antagain/iStockphoto; 2 (frog cr): GlobalP/iStockphoto; 3 (frog): Kikkerdirk/ Dreamstime; 3 (background): Talisalex/Dreamstime; 4–5 (water): IgorKovalchuk/iStockphoto; 4 (green frog, grass): Ir717/Dreamstime; 4 (edible frog): Kikkerdirk/Dreamstime; 4 (African clawed frog): GlobalP/iStockphoto; 4 (tree frog, stem): Leksele/Dreamstime; 4 (ornate horned frog): Amwu/Dreamstime; 4 (cartoon frog, used throughout): sldesign78/ iStockphoto; 5 (red-eyed tree frog, stem): alptraum/iStockphoto; 5 (plant r): Ancher/ Dreamstime; 5 (poison dart frog): Kikkerdirk/iStockphoto; 5 (glass frog): Snowleopard1/ iStockphoto; 5 (marsh frog): GlobalP/iStockphoto; 5 (Imbabura tree frog): Kikkerdirk/ Dreamstime; 5 (bullfrog): stevelenzphoto/iStockphoto; 5 (Malayan horned frog): GlobalP/ iStockphoto; 6–7 (main image): Michael Durham/Minden Pictures/Getty Images; 6cl: Photowitch/Dreamstime; 6bl: AlasdairJames/iStockphoto; 6 (tape, used throughout): spxChrome/iStockphoto; 7br: Birgit Kremer/www.iberia-natur.com; 8–9 (main image): ABDESIGN/iStockphoto; 8cl: spxChrome/iStockphoto; 9tl: Alptraum/Dreamstime; 9cr: Isselee/Dreamstime; 9bc: Atelopus/iStockphoto; 10–11 (sky): Tan4ikk/Dreamstime; 10–11 (water surface): Bestmoose/Dreamstime; 10–11 (underwater): Rike_/iStockphoto; 10–11 (leaping frog): Stephen Dalton/Science Source; 10–11 (swimming frog): Antagain/ iStockphoto; 10 (duck): Thomas Seybold/iStockphoto; 10 (otter): A-Digit/iStockphoto; 11tr: GlobalP/iStockphoto; 10 (penguin): rikidoh/iStockphoto; 11 (human): 4x6/iStockphoto; 12–13 (background, green frog in water): Photomo/Dreamstime; 12 (poison dart frogs l to r): Kikkerdirk/iStockphoto, GlobalP/iStockphoto, Pixie Chick/Fotolia, Kikkerdirk/iStockphoto; 12bc: Lanalanglois/Dreamstime; 13tl: Stephen J. Krasemann/All Canada Photos/SuperStock; 13tr: KeithSzafranski/iStockphoto; 13bl: Alslutsky/Dreamstime; 13bc: Mshuffy/Dreamstime; 13br: Gabbro/Alamy Images; 14–15 (main image): Oktay Ortakcioglu/iStockphoto; 15 (background): Biansho/Dreamstime; 15 (lily pads): Manasapat/Dreamstime; 15 (frog t): Animals Animals/SuperStock; 15 (flower): pixonaut/iStockphoto; 15 (frog c): irin717/ iStockphoto; 15 (frog body): Tom McHugh/Science Source; 15 (frog b): Antagain/ iStockphoto; 16–17 (sky): Tan4ikk/Dreamstime; 16–17 (underwater): Melking/Dreamstime; 16 (adult frog): jesue92/iStockphoto; 16 (eggs): Isselee/Dreamstime; 16 (tadpoles): GlobalP/iStockphoto; 16 (butterfly): SongSpeckels/ iStockphoto; 16 (bee): bubaone/iStockphoto; 17 (tadpole, froglet): GlobalP/iStockphoto; 17 (adult frog): Jgade/Dreamstime; 17 (ladybug): bubaone/iStockphoto; 17 (crab): rangepuppies/iStockphoto; 18–19t: Minden Pictures/SuperStock; 18–19 (background b): Lequint/Dreamstime; 18 (toad): Minden Pictures/SuperStock; 18 (rock): princessdlaf/ iStockphoto; 19bl: Minden Pictures/SuperStock; 19br: Kikkerdirk/iStockphoto; 20–21 (map): Jezper/Shutterstock; 20 (wood frog): Donyanedomam/

Dreamstime; 20 (bullfrog): cavefish/iStockphoto; 20 (bullfrog background): DRB Images, LLC/ iStockphoto; 20 (poison dart frog): mashabuba/iStockphoto; 20 (poison dart frog background): szefei/iStockphoto; 20 (desert rain frog): Arie van der Meijden/CalPhotos/ University of California, Berkeley; 20 (desert rain frog background): Piccaya/Dreamstime; 21tr: Kikkerdirk/Fotolia; 21 (agile frog): Chatroux André/Wikipedia; 21 (agile frog background): johnPkrause/iStockphoto; 21 (corroboree frog): ANT Photo Library/Science Source; 21 (corroboree frog background): Fitzo/iStockphoto; 21 (Wallace's flying frog): Stephen Dalton/ Science Source; 21 (Wallace's flying frog background): Joegough/Dreamstime; 22–23 (main image): Minden Pictures/SuperStock; 22–23 (background): Wtolenaars/Dreamstime; 24–25 (background): ricardoazoury/iStockphoto; 24tl: -1001-/iStockphoto; 24cl: Thomas Marent/ Visuals Unlimited/Getty Images; 24cr: Brian Gratwicke/Wikipedia; 24bl: John_Woodcock/ iStockphoto; 24br: aleksandr-mansurov-ru/iStockphoto; 25cl: Michael J. Tyler/Science Source; 25bl: kathykonkle/iStockphoto; 25 (frog r): Cathykeifer/Dreamstime; 25 (leaf br): Kikkerdirk/Dreamstime; 26–27 (background): Shariffc/Dreamstime; 26b: Fletcher & Baylis/ Science Source; 27tl: Kevin Tildsley/Planetary Visions Ltd.; 27tr: Fletcher & Baylis/Science Source; 27cl, 27cr: Rainforest Rescue International; 27b: Fletcher & Baylis/Science Source; 28 (#1): Isselee/Dreamstime; 28 (#2): Mgkuijpers/Dreamstime; 28 (#3 t): Minden Pictures/ SuperStock; 28 (#3 bl): Cattallina/iStockphoto; 28 (#3 br): hypergon/iStockphoto; 28 (#4 l): AskinTulayOver/iStockphoto; 28 (#4 r): Rittmeyer EN, Allison A, Gründler MC, Thompson DK, Austin CC/Wikipedia; 28 (#5): ABDESIGN/iStockphoto; 29 (#6): GlobalP/iStockphoto; 29 (#7): higyou/iStockphoto; 29 (#8 t): Corey Hochachka/Media Bakery; 29 (#8 b): kathykonkle/ iStockphoto; 29 (#9 t): hypergon/iStockphoto; 29 (#9 b): A-Digit/iStockphoto; 29cr: tunart/ iStockphoto; 29 (#10): Rex Cauldwell; 30–31 (background, frog tr): Spanishalex/Dreamstime; 32 (bamboo): Youths/Dreamstime; 32 (frog t): Sebastian Duda/Fotolia; 32 (frog br): Carolinasmith/Dreamstime; 32 (lily pad): Manasapat/Dreamstime.

Cover
Front cover: (leaf icon) liquidplanet/iStockphoto; (main image) Thomas Marent; (background b) Jasmina007/iStockphoto. Back cover: (tr) Amwu/Dreamstime; (computer monitor) Manaemedia/Dreamstime. Inside front cover: (leaves) olegganko/iStockphoto; (frogs t) kathykonkle/iStockphoto; (frog br) hypergon/iStockphoto.

Thank you
For their generosity of time in sharing their expertise, special thanks to Charith Senanayake, Director of Rainforest Rescue International (www.rainforestrescueinternational.org), and Kim Dennis-Bryan, PhD.

SCHOLASTIC discover more readers™

Frogs are small, but they make a big noise. Meet some of the cutest and the craziest!

Get ready for a world of information for readers at every level.

LEVEL 1
Beginning readers
Learning to read for information
- 200–500 words
- simple sentences
- new vocabulary
- key facts
- first infographics
- famous people

LEVEL 2
Developing readers
Starting to read for information
- 500–1,200 words
- more complex sentences
- challenging vocabulary
- infographics
- maps and charts
- quotes from experts

LEVEL 3
Independent readers
Reading fluently for information
- 1,000–1,800 words
- complex text structures
- technical vocabulary
- maps, charts, and time lines
- expert quotes and debates
- varied writing styles

Download your free digital activities for more reading fun!

Visit www.scholastic.com/discovermore/readers

APPEALS TO 1ST–2ND GRADERS

READING LEVEL GRADE 2

More leveling information for this book:
www.scholastic.com/readinglevel

$3.99 US / $4.99 CAN

ISBN 978-0-545-57271-2

EAN

9 780545 572712

50399

REGIS COLLEGE LIBRARY

3 1761 04835 3411

Susan K. Wood

Spiritual Exegesis

and the Church

in the Theology of

Henri

de Lubac